Conference Planner, Agenda, Organizer, Notes

Conference

Date

Name: _____

Company: _____

Phone #: _____

Email: _____

Travel Information

Dates: _____

Flight #: _____ Flight #: _____

Departure Time: _____ Arrival Time: _____

Departure City: _____ Arrival City: _____

Hotel: _____

_____

Hotel Contact: _____

Car Rental: _____

_____

Conference Venue(s)/Address: _____

_____

_____

_____

To Do:

Goals/Ideas:

Conference Overview

TIME	Day 1	Day 2	Day 3
8:00am			
9:00am			
10:00am			
11:00am			
12:00pm			
1:00pm			
2:00pm			
3:00pm			
4:00pm			
5:00pm			
6:00pm			
7:00pm			
8:00pm			

Conference Overview

TIME	Day 4	Day 5	NOTES
8:00am			
9:00am			
10:00am			
11:00am			
12:00pm			
1:00pm			
2:00pm			
3:00pm			
4:00pm			
5:00pm			
6:00pm			
7:00pm			
8:00pm			

TIME	Day 1
8:00am	
9:00am	
10:00am	
11:00am	
12:00pm	
1:00pm	
2:00pm	
3:00pm	
4:00pm	
5:00pm	
6:00pm	
7:00pm	
8:00pm	

Conference Notes

Awesome People/Follow Up

Meetings

Goals:

Conference Notes

Conference Notes

Conference Notes

Conference Notes

Conference Notes

Conference Notes

TIME	Day 2
8:00am	
9:00am	
10:00am	
11:00am	
12:00pm	
1:00pm	
2:00pm	
3:00pm	
4:00pm	
5:00pm	
6:00pm	
7:00pm	
8:00pm	

Conference Notes

Awesome People/Follow Up

Meetings

Goals:

Conference Notes

Conference Notes

Conference Notes

Conference Notes

Conference Notes

TIME	Day 3
8:00am	
9:00am	
10:00am	
11:00am	
12:00pm	
1:00pm	
2:00pm	
3:00pm	
4:00pm	
5:00pm	
6:00pm	
7:00pm	
8:00pm	

Conference Notes

Awesome People/Follow Up

Meetings

Goals:

Conference Notes

Conference Notes

Conference Notes

Conference Notes

Conference Notes

TIME	Day 4
8:00am	
9:00am	
10:00am	
11:00am	
12:00pm	
1:00pm	
2:00pm	
3:00pm	
4:00pm	
5:00pm	
6:00pm	
7:00pm	
8:00pm	

Conference Notes

Awesome People/Follow Up

Meetings

Goals:

Conference Notes

Conference Notes

Conference Notes

Conference Notes

Conference Notes

TIME	Day 5
8:00am	
9:00am	
10:00am	
11:00am	
12:00pm	
1:00pm	
2:00pm	
3:00pm	
4:00pm	
5:00pm	
6:00pm	
7:00pm	
8:00pm	

Conference Notes

Awesome People/Follow Up

Meetings

Goals:

Conference Notes

Conference Notes

Conference Notes

Conference Notes

Conference Notes

www.ingramcontent.com/pod-product-compliance
Lightning Source LLC
Chambersburg PA
CBHW040227040426
42331CB00041B/3501